FUSION WITH BISTRO 430

A Cookbook by
Bistro 430 Enterprises, LLC
Generously supported by
Wintberg Inc.

Copyright © 2015 by Bistro 430 Enterprises, LLC.

All rights reserved. No part of this book may be reproduced in any form without prior written permission of publisher and author. No responsibility is accepted by producer, publisher, or printer for any infringement of copyright or otherwise, arising from the contents of this publication.

ISBN: 978-0-9861038-0-3

Printed in the United States of America

Cover, Art Direction, and Food Design by Ken Francis
Bistro 430 Enterprises, LLC
Austin, Texas 78701
www.bistro430.com

Publisher, Project Management and Graphic Services by Wintberg Inc
Wintberg Inc.
Las Vegas, Nevada 89107
www.wintberginc.com

Food Photography by Julian Francis Sr.
For information about special discounts on bulk purchasing, please contact Wintberg Inc at Productsales@wintberginc.com

Notes for the Reader
This book uses imperial, metric, and U.S. cup measurements. Follow the same units of measurement throughout; do not mix imperial and metric.

The times given are an approximate guide only. Preparation times differ according to the technique used by different people and the cooking times may also vary from those given.
Sufferers from nut allergies should be aware that some of the ready-made ingredients used in the recipes in this book may contain nuts to include the recipe. Always check the packaging or recipe before use.

Dedication

To family and friends, mentors in the kitchen, and veterans. Thank you for all the love and support.

*So we may teach others, support your passion,
and mentor always - Ken Francis*

TEN TIPS FOR CREATING A GREAT MEAL

- Start with confidence

- Always Invest in good sharp knives

- Shop fresh, for only what you need

- Most times Salt and Pepper is all you need

- Store ingredients properly

- Always make sure pan is hot

- Have the store deli, seafood or meat counters do most of the cutting

- Buying whole chickens has many great uses and can be cost effective

- Small plastic deli containers are great for storing ingredients

- Make cooking fun, and not a spectator sport. Encourage others to be a part of creating a great meal by assigning them a recipe!

- Bonus Tip: Well prepared stocks and sauces can make a difference

Foreword and Introduction

What's included in this book:

Throughout this book, we have created a fusion of mouth watering recipes from different regional and national cuisines to create tasty soups, snacks, and main dishes. As a long time enthusiastic home cook and professional, I have seen many cookbooks. But only a few really catch my eye in simplicity and preparing meals for vegetarians, meat lovers and who can forget the sweet heart desserts.

This book was designed for those with little to no cooking skills. Best of all, we have added a bit of extra flavor by including wine suggestions with each dish - although personal taste should be the first criteria in wine selection.

We have thoroughly tested recipe after recipe to ensure that you get the absolute best experience when sharing with family and friends. After all, that's what this book is about Fun and Sharing.

Try our Horseradish Risotto or Cardamom Ice cream on a Danish butter cookie. I must say it is delicious. If you have a passion for entertaining family and friends with good food this book is for you. Thank you in advance and we hope you enjoy for many years to come.

Ken Francis

President and Co-founder

Bistro 430 Enterprises, LLC

Recipe Testing 2013 - Pork Belly with Chives Gnocchi's and Baby Carrots

CONTENTS

INTRODUCTION

9

APPETIZERS

13

SMALL PLATES

31

MAIN DISHES

49

DESSERTS

65

INDEX

89

SALADS

ROASTED BEET SALAD WITH MACADAMIA NUT VINAIGRETTE

DILL CHICKEN SALAD WITH POMEGRANATE VINAIGRETTE

SOUPS

STRAWBERRY GAZPACHO

BUTTERNUT SQUASH SOUP

MUSSEL SOUP

SNACKS

SPICED MARCONA

TOASTED DATES WITH SEA SALT

ROASTED MINI SWEET PEPPERS

APPETIZERS

APPETIZERS – SALAD

Roasted Beet Salad with Macadamia Nut Vinaigrette

Roasting beets can intensify their flavor, bring out the earthy sweetness, and peeling of the outer skin so much easier. Beets are particularly delicious as a salad accompanied by the zest of orange and tanginess of goat or feta cheese.
Wine pairing: Pinot Noir

ROASTED BEET SALAD WITH MACADAMIA NUT VINAIGRETTE

Serve: 4   Prep time: 20 Minutes   Cook time: 50 Minutes

Roasted Beets

1/2 pound Red Beets
1/2 pound Golden Beets
1/2 pound Chioggia Beets (optional)

Method: Preheat oven to 375° F (190°C). Wrap beets in foil and place on baking sheet to catch any juice. Roast beets for 40 to 50 minutes. If beets are starting to dry out or looking scorched pour water over them before re-wrapping. Beets are ready when fork tender.

Transfer and cool immediately. Allow beets to cool slightly, before removing the skin.

Herb Salad

1 bunch Fresh Cilantro
1 bunch Fresh Parsley
1 bunch Mint Leaves
2 ounces Goat cheese or crumbled Feta
1 Orange, supremed

Method: Remove stems on herbs up to 1/2 inch. Do not mix herbs together until ready to plate.

Macadamia Nut Vinaigrette

1 large Shallot, finely chopped
1 Tablespoon Orange Blossom Honey
1 teaspoon Red Pepper Flakes
2 Tablespoons Fresh Cilantro. Chopped
1/2 Cup Passion Fruit Puree
1/2 teaspoon Kosher Salt
1/2 Cup Extra Virgin Olive Oil
1/4 Cup Macadamia Nuts

Method: In a blender or food processor combine the first "Six" ingredients. Blend until smooth. With machine running, add oil in a slow, steady stream.

Turn off the machine; Add macadamia nuts, and pulse until nuts are finely chopped. Vinaigrette should be a creamy texture not a paste. If needed, add more puree or oil and pulse to consistency.

The Finish

Slice beets 1/8 inch thick, brush a Tablespoon of vinaigrette on each plate, then arrange 6 Beet slices horizontally across plate with overlap. Top off with a bed of herb salad. Serve with orange and cheese.

HINTS AND TIPS : COVER HANDS WITH COOKING OIL TO PREVENT BEET JUICE STAIN

APPETIZERS – SALAD

Dill Chicken Salad with Pomegranate Vinaigrette

The peppery taste of Arugula is intensified with candied pecans and pomegranate. The warmth of the Dill crusted chicken offers a needed change in texture, temperature and flavor especially comforting when combined with spinach.
Wine pairing: Chardonnay

DILL CHICKEN SALAD WITH POMEGRANATE VINAIGRETTE

Serve: 4   Prep time: 2 Hours   Cook time: 40 Minutes

Dill Chicken

2 ounces Fresh Dill, chopped
1 Cup Buttermilk
2 Tablespoons Kosher Salt
2 pounds Chicken Breast, cut into 1/2 inch cubes
1/2 Cup Bread crumbs for breading
2 Egg yolks, beaten and lighten with 1 teaspoon of water
Canola oil for pan frying

Method: In a large bowl, combine half the dill with buttermilk, add 1 Tablespoon salt. Add chicken cubes and refrigerate overnight or at least for 2 hours.

In a medium pan or deep fryer, heat oil until 350°F (176°C). Pat dry the chicken. Beat eggs in a shallow dish or bowl. Dredge chicken pieces in the egg, then place in a bag with the remaining dill and bread crumbs. Seal bag and shake to coat. Transfer chicken to hot oil and cook for about 5 to 7 minutes until golden brown or juices run clear. Remove from oil; Serve or keep warm.

Pomegranate Vinaigrette

1 Cup Pomegranate Concentrate
3 ounces Red Wine Vinegar
2 Tablespoons Honey
1 Cup Extra Virgin Olive oil
Salt and Pepper to Taste

Method: In a blender or food processor, combine first "three" ingredients, pulse for 30 seconds, then slowly add oil; Season to taste with salt and pepper. Use as needed.

Arugula Salad

1/2 pound Fresh Arugula, trimmed
1/2 pound Spinach, trimmed
2 Cups Candied Pecans (See page 77)
1/2 Cup Pickled Onions (See page 78)

Method: Wash and spin dry Arugula and Spinach. Combine ingredients in a small bowl with a drizzle of vinaigrette.

The Finish

On a warm serving plate, spoon a teaspoon of vinaigrette in the center of each plate, place a bed of salad across plate. Top off with 5 to 6 chicken pieces. Garnish with more candied pecans and pickled onions. Serve warm.

HINTS AND TIPS: IF YOU PREFER, USE FLOUR AT THE START OF THE BREADING PROCESS TO PROVIDE THE EGGS SOMETHING TO CLING AGAINST

APPETIZERS – SOUP

Strawberry Gazpacho

A rare twist to the traditional Spanish tomato base soup. Gazpacho is a cold savory soup great for the hot summer months. Surprisingly this dish is not sweet, but light and refreshing with a delicate balance of flavors.
Wine pairing: Sparkling wine or Mimosa

STRAWBERRY GAZPACHO

Serve: 4   Prep time: 4 Hours   Cook time: 0 Minutes

Gazpacho

3 pounds Strawberries, hulled and quartered
1 Cup Red Onion, chopped
1 Cup Red Bell Pepper, chopped
1/4 Jalapeño Pepper, seeded and chopped
1 Cucumber, peeled, seeded, and diced
1 Clove Garlic, crushed
Sprig Fresh Tarragon
2 Mint leaves, chopped
1/4 Cup Red Wine Vinegar
1/2 Cup Extra Virgin Olive Oil
Pinch of Salt
1 Cup Vegetable Stock

Method: In a large bowl using your hands, mix together strawberries, onion, peppers, cucumber, garlic, tarragon, vinegar, mint and olive oil; Cover with plastic wrap and refrigerate for at least 3 hours – best overnight.

Transfer mixture to a blender; blend until smooth. Taste for seasoning. If mixture is too thick add some stock. Transfer to a bowl and refrigerate for at least 1 hour before serving.

Garnish

1/2 Cup Red Bell Pepper, small diced
1/2 Cup Green Bell Pepper, small diced
1/2 Cup Cucumber, small diced
1 Avocado, small diced
2 Tablespoons Red Onion, small diced

Method: Keep ingredients separated for later use. When serving, divide ingredients evenly among the individual serving bowls. The key is to build height in the center of the bowl with garnish - as shown below.

The Finish

Using the chilled bowls with garnish, pour or ladle about 1 to 2 cups of soup in each bowl. Drizzle with a little olive oil and serve immediately.

HINTS AND TIPS : GAZPACHO TASTE BETTER SERVED COLD. THE FLAVOR IMPROVES WHEN LEFT OVERNIGHT. ROOM TEMPERATURE BOWLS ARE OK IF THE SOUP IS CHILLED PROPERLY

APPETIZER – SOUP

Roasted Butternut Squash Soup

Roasting squash in the oven can add flavor and this one is a crowd pleaser. A must have elegant soup with a sweet and savory flavor. Perfect as an appetizer or serve as a full meal.
Wine pairing: Chardonnay, Riesling, Chianti

ROASTED BUTTERNUT SQUASH SOUP

Serve: 4   Prep time: 20 Minutes   Cook time: 40 Minutes

Butternut Squash

2 Tablespoons Butter, unsalted
1 small Yellow Onion, chopped
1 Stalk Celery, chopped
1 medium Carrot, chopped
1 large Butternut Squash, peeled, seeded, and cubed
1 Cup Heavy Cream
1/4 teaspoon of Nutmeg, ground
1/4 teaspoon Cloves, ground
2 Cups Chicken or Vegetable stock
Salt and Pepper to Taste

Method: Preheat oven to 350°F (176°C). In a medium pot, melt 1 Tablespoon butter. Add half the onion, celery, and carrot. Cook about 3 minutes until vegetables soften and become lightly translucent. Stir in the squash and let cook for 3 minutes. Season with salt and pepper. Reserving pot for later, use a rubber spatula and transfer ingredients to a large roasting pan or baking tray. Spread out in a single layer. Roast in oven for 15 to 20 minutes (stirring every 10 minutes) until outside of the squash is light brown and center is fork tender. Remove from oven.

In the medium pot, bring cream and 1/2 Cup of stock to a simmer. Add remaining butter and onion. Stir to combine. Add the roasted ingredients from oven to the pot, season with nutmeg, cloves, and continue to simmer for 10 minutes until squash is falling apart. Add more stock if needed.

Remove from heat and allow to cool slightly. Carefully using a blender or immersion blender "Puree" soup slowly adding more stock until smooth. Strain soup to remove any remaining vegetable fibers. Return soup to the pot on low heat. Keep warm and serve immediately.

The Finish

In warm serving bowls, Ladle 4 to 6 ounces of soup into each bowl. Garnish with tarragon leaves and serve with Crème Fraiche (optional) - See recipe on page 77.

HINTS AND TIPS: PUREE SOUP IN PORTIONS RATHER THAN ALL AT ONCE, ESPECIALLY IF THE BLENDER IS NOT LARGE ENOUGH - PREVENTS SPILLOVER

APPETIZER – SOUP

Mussel Soup

Garlic, shallots, parsley, and a bit of cayenne just a nice rich flavor needed for fresh mussels. Highly suggested to always scrub mussels and remove any beards.
Wine pairing: Chardonnay, Sauvignon Blanc, Muscadet

MUSSEL SOUP

Serve: 4   Prep time: 15 Minutes   Cook time: 30 Minutes

Ingredients

1 Tablespoon Butter, unsalted
1 Shallot, finely chopped
2 Cloves Garlic, finely chopped
2 pounds Mussels in shell, uncooked
1 Cup dry White Wine
2 Cups Fish or Vegetable stock

Method: Discard any mussels that remain opened. Scrape off barnacles "beards" and scrub the mussels thoroughly with a stiff brush under cold running water; Drain.

In a medium sauté pan over medium-low heat, melt butter, add shallot and garlic. Stir until shallot become soft but do not burn the garlic. Carefully, add the mussels, white wine and stock; Cover with lid and bring to a boil. Cook for about 3 to 5 minutes shaking occasionally.

Remove lid and discard any mussels that remain closed. Transfer the remaining mussels from the liquid with a slotted spoon into a large dish or bowl. Make broth using the same pan.

The Finish

Broth

1 Tablespoons Butter, unsalted
2 Cups Heavy cream
Pinch of Cayenne, ground
Kosher Salt
Freshly Ground Black Pepper

Method: After removing the mussels, add butter and the cream. Bring to a boil, stirring occasionally over high heat for about 1 minute to combine. (If pan starts to boil over, remove from heat and stir). Liquid should start to thicken slightly.

Lower heat to medium low, then add the cayenne, season with salt and pepper to taste. Return mussels to the warm pan and turn off the heat. Serve immediately.

Garnish

1 Tablespoon Fresh parsley, chopped
1/2 French Baguette, enough to get 8 slices 1/4 inch thick, toasted

Using a slotted spoon or kitchen tong, divide mussels between serving bowls about 8 to 12 cooked mussels each. Pour hot broth over mussels and garnish with parsley. Serve immediately with baguette slices 2 per guest.

HINTS AND TIPS : BE SURE TO CLEAN MUSSELS AND DISCARD ANY THAT DO NOT OPEN, CONSUMING MAY CAUSE SERIOUS FOOD ILLNESS

APPETIZERS – SNACKS

Spiced Marcona

Great snack to have for those scotch or beer occasions. The obvious nutty flavor of almonds combined with the sweet smoky spice of cumin and paprika drives this dish home.
Drink pairing: Single Malt Scotch or Lager

SPICED MARCONA

Serve: 8 Prep time: 10 Minutes Cook time: 40 Minutes

Ingredients

1 large Egg white
1 Tablespoon Water
1/2 Cup Brown Sugar
1 Tablespoon Cumin, ground
1 teaspoon Paprika, Spanish
1 teaspoon Kosher Salt
1/4 teaspoon Cayenne Pepper
1 pound Marcona or raw Whole Almonds (blanched)

Garnish

1 Tablespoon Fresh parsley or herb mixture (dill, parsley, thyme, cilantro and basil), chopped

Method: Preheat oven to 275°F (135°C). Coat a large baking sheet with cooking spray or use a Silpat.

In a medium stainless steel bowl, whisk together the egg white and water until frothy. In a separate bowl, combine the sugar, cumin, paprika, salt and cayenne.

Place almonds in egg mixture and toss to coat completely. Remove almonds and strain off any excess egg white. Transfer almonds to the bowl with the spices, toss thoroughly until almonds are well coated. Remove from spices and spread out evenly on the baking sheet.

Bake almonds for about 20 minutes, stir and continue to bake for an additional 20 minutes or until the almonds are dry and lightly golden. Remove from the oven, and transfer to a rack or counter for cooling. Set aside for 7 to 10 minutes before serving.

The Finish

Arrange almonds on a serving tray or dish garnished with paprika and chopped herbs.

HINTS AND TIPS: STORE PROPERLY IN AN AIR TIGHT CONTAINER TO ENSURE FRESHNESS FOR LATER USE.

APPETIZERS – SNACKS

Sautéed Medjool Dates with Sea Salt

Dates and Sea salt was a game changer for me. The warmth and sweetness of this tree fruit with a slight salty finish will leave your guest wanting more.
Wine pairing: Muscat or Pinot Grigio

SAUTÉED MEDJOOL DATES WITH SEA SALT

Serve: 4   Prep time: 10 Minutes   Cook time: 10 Minutes

Ingredients

12 ounces Medjool Dates

Extra Virgin Olive Oil

1 Tablespoon Fresh Parsley, chopped

Sea Salt

Method: With a sharp knife, make a small incision on one side of the dates to remove pits. After removing the pit, gently close the incision by squeezing on both sides of the date.

Heat the oil in a medium sauté pan over medium-high heat. Add the dates and toss to coat. Sauté the dates for about 1 to 2 minutes until dates start to brown slightly. With a slotted spoon or kitchen tong gently remove dates from the pan and serve warm.

Alternative cooking method: Dates can be sautéed for 30 to 40 seconds on medium high heat and place into an oven at 400°F (204°C) for about 1 minute to ensure the dates are completely warm through.

The Finish

While dates are still warm season with sea salt. Place the dates onto a serving platter or plate, top with a little parsley and serve warm.

HINTS AND TIPS: BE SURE TO REFRIGERATE DATES AFTER OPENING PACKAGE. COMPLETELY WARM DATES THROUGH FOR A BETTER MOUTH FEEL

APPETIZERS – SNACKS

ROASTED MINI SWEET PEPPERS

This delicate treat goes from snappy to luscious, sweet to tangy and will explode on your palate all at once. Roasting then steaming peppers helps to make them more enjoyable by softening the texture. **Wine Pairing: Pinot Gris**

ROASTED MINI SWEET PEPPERS

Serve: 8   Prep time: 20 Minutes   Cook time: 40 Minutes

Roasted Peppers

2 pounds Sweet Mini-Peppers
1/2 Cup Canola or Olive oil
Pinch of Kosher Salt

Method: Preheat the oven to 375°F (190°C). In a roasting pan or dish, lightly drizzle peppers with oil or use cooking spray to coat.

Transfer to oven and roast peppers for about 25 to 40 minutes until skin is soft and slightly chard - turn peppers occasionally. While peppers are roasting prepare the filling.

Remove peppers from oven and cover with lid or foil allowing peppers to steam for 10 minutes. Uncover and drain oil from dish into sauce pan to make sauce. Allow peppers to cool slightly before making a small incision on the side of each pepper to remove seeds and fill.

Dipping Sauce

Oil Remaining from Roasted peppers
1 small Shallot, finely chopped
1 Clove Garlic, finely chopped
Pinch of Cayenne Pepper
2 Tablespoons Honey
1 Cup Heavy cream

Method: In a small sauce pan over medium heat combine shallot, garlic and cayenne. Turn heat to medium-low and add honey and cream. Stir; Reduce until the sauce is a creamy thick consistency or "Nappe" about 5 minutes.

Goat Cheese Filling

12 ounces Chevre 'Goat cheese'
1 bunch Chives, shaved

Allow the goat cheese to sit at room temperature for 10 to 15 minutes. In a medium bowl, combine cheese and chives using the back of a spoon. Place mixture in a pastry bag or zip-lock and secure opening to fill peppers.

The Finish

Arrange peppers onto a serving tray or plate. Garnish with parsley and serve with dipping sauce. Refrigerate if not serving immediately.

HINTS AND TIPS: ROASTING AND STEAMING ALLOW PEPPERS TO RETAIN NUTRIENTS, FLAVOR AND COLOR. REMOVING THE SKIN IS OPTIONAL

SMALL PLATES

SMALL BITES

PROSCIUTTO, FIGS, AND CAPERS

TOMATO BRUSCHETTA

VEGETARIAN

ROASTED BROCCOLI AND BRUSSEL SPROUTS

TOMATO AVOCADO DELIGHT

SEAFOOD

SEARED AHI TUNA

SEAFOOD PAELLA

MEATS

BACON, CAPERS, BRAISED GREENS FLAT BREAD

PAN-SEARED SLICED BEEF WITH GREEN BEANS

SMALL PLATES – BITES

PROSCIUTTO, FIGS, AND CAPERS

Delicate aroma of prosciutto intensified with the flavor of mint, sweetness of figs and the saltiness of capers. Perfect for any gathering.
Wine pairing: Beaujolais, Pinot Noir

PROSCIUTTO, FIGS, AND CAPERS

Serve: 8   Prep time: 15 Minutes   Cook time: 7 Minutes

Ingredients

4 ounces Prosciutto, very thinly sliced
8 Whole Wheat bread for base, toasted
10 Figs, sliced 1/4 inch thick
1 Tablespoon Capers, drained

3 Mint leaves, fine chiffonade
Extra Virgin Olive Oil

Method: Preheat oven to 250°F (121°C). On a baking sheet, arrange bread in a single layer. Gently brush oil onto one side of the bread. Toast bread - oil side up for 5 to 7 minutes until slightly brown. Cut or mold out medium circles about 3 inches in diameter to make the base. Enough to take one bite. You should be able to get two bases per slice if you start in the corner.

Top the base with 3 pieces of fig, add the capers and then layer with a bed of prosciutto building height. Drizzle with olive oil and garnish with mint leaves.

 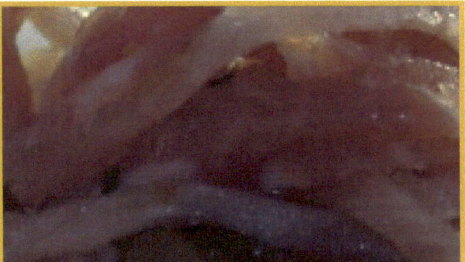 

The Finish

Divide the delicious bites amongst the guest or use a serving platter. Serve slightly warm or at room temperature.

HINTS AND TIPS: ADD A LIGHT CHEESE SPREAD TO THE BASE LAYER.

SMALL PLATES – BITES

TOMATO BRUSCHETTA

Try some mouth watering diced tomatoes on a toasted baguette with grated Parmesan. Tomato seeds can be slight bitter and the skin hard to digest. Removing the skin and seeds can offer a more fresh and palatable experience.
Wine pairing: Chardonnay, Sauvignon Blanc

TOMATO BRUSCHETTA

Serve: 8   Prep time: 90 Minutes   Cook time: 10 Minutes

Ingredients

2 pounds (about 6 or 7) Roma Tomatoes,
2 Tablespoons Fresh Basil or Fresh Parsley, minced
2 Clove Garlic, minced
3 Tablespoons Extra Virgin Olive Oil
1 teaspoon Kosher Salt
1/4 teaspoon Fresh Ground Black Pepper

Method: Bring a pot of water to a boil. Wash and rinse tomatoes. Remove the stem (if it has one), flip it over and cut an "X" into the bottom. Don't cut too deeply — just enough to score the skin.

Add tomatoes to the pot, Blanch for 15 to 30 seconds. Use a slotted spoon to transfer tomatoes from pot to a bowl of ice water. After 30 seconds, remove the skin of the tomatoes, cut in halves and remove seeds. Small dice and ensure to remove any additional seeds found.

In a medium bowl, combine tomatoes, herb, garlic and Extra Virgin Olive Oil. Season with salt and pepper; mix thoroughly. Chill for at least 1 hour or best overnight before serving.

Base

1/2 French Baguette
2 Tablespoons Fresh garlic, minced

Method: Preheat oven to 450°F (230°C). Using a bread knife cut the baguette on the diagonal into 1/2 inch thick slices. Brush or drizzle oil on one side of each slice.

Arrange on baking sheet in a single layer oil-side down. Toast the bread slices about 5 to 6 minutes until golden brown. Remove bread from oven and set aside to cool for 5 minutes before topping with tomato mixture.

Garnish

2 Tablespoons Parmesan, grated

The Finish

Using a spoon, top each toasted slice with the tomato mixture. Drizzle with a little olive oil and garnish with a sprinkle of Parmesan. Serve using a platter or individual plates.

HINTS AND TIPS: PREPARE MIXTURE THE DAY BEFORE AND CHILL OVERNIGHT. THIS ALLOWS THE FLAVOR TO FULLY MARINATE AND DEVELOP

SMALL PLATES – VEGETARIAN

ROASTED GARLIC BROCCOLI AND BRUSSELS SPROUTS

Lightly caramelizing vegetables before roasting is a great way to pull additional flavor out of the vegetable.
Wine pairing: Viognier, Pinot Noir

ROASTED GARLIC BROCCOLI AND BRUSSELS SPROUTS

Serve: 8 Prep time: 10 Minutes Cook time: 20 Minutes

Ingredients

2 pounds Broccoli Florets, trimmed
1 Tablespoon Olive Oil or Canola blend
2 Cloves Garlic, minced
1 teaspoon Red Pepper Flakes
1 pound Brussels sprouts, trimmed and halved
Kosher Salt
Fresh Ground Black Pepper

Method: Preheat oven to 350°F (176°C). Prepare a roasting dish with Silpat or apply cooking spray.

Bring a 2 quart pot of water to a boil. Blanch the broccoli for 20 to 30 seconds. Remove from pot, strain and drain. Transfer to a roasting dish and set aside.

In a large sauté pan, heat oil over medium heat. Add the garlic and red pepper flakes; Cook for 30 seconds. Add the Brussels sprouts cut side down. Let sit in pan and caramelized for about 30 to 40 seconds depending on the size of vegetable. Transfer to roasting dish with broccoli.

Season ingredients with salt and pepper. Place in oven and roast for 5 to 10 minutes until vegetables are fork tender. Remove from oven and serve immediately.

Croutons

1/2 French bread, cut into 1/2 inch cubes
1 Tablespoon Parsley, chopped
2 Tablespoons Olive Oil
Kosher Salt
Fresh Ground Black Pepper

Method: In a medium bowl, toss bread cubes in olive oil, parsley, salt and pepper. Coat evenly.

With oven at 350°F (176°C) and using a baking sheet, spread out the bread cubes into a single layer.

Bake for 10 to 15 minutes or until golden brown. The crouton will harden as they cool.

Store any remaining croutons in an air tight container for future use.

The Finish

To serve, place vegetables in serving bowls or plates. Serve warm with croutons.

HINTS AND TIPS: ADDING BUTTER AND ZEST CAN ADD A BALANCE OF FLAVOR TO THIS DISH

SMALL PLATES - VEGETARIAN

Tomato Avocado Delight

This delicious and savory dish is enticing as an appetizer, small plate or full meal during the summer months.
Wine pairing: Sauvignon Blanc, Chardonnay

TOMATO AVOCADO DELIGHT

Serve: 6   Prep time: 40 Minutes   Cook time: 0 Minutes

Ingredients

2 large Round Tomatoes, sliced 1/4 inch thick
2 Tablespoons Fresh Parsley, minced
2 Tablespoons Fresh Basil, Minced
2 Tablespoons Fresh Mint, Minced
1 teaspoon Kosher Salt
1/2 teaspoon Freshly Ground Black Pepper
1/2 Cup Extra Virgin Olive Oil

Method: Using a sharp knife, slice the tomatoes and avocados. On a flat surface or baking sheet, sprinkle tomatoes evenly with parsley, basil and mint. Season with salt and pepper. Drizzle with oil.

Refrigerate for at least 30 minutes. Meanwhile, prepare garnish.

Garnish

3 ounces Asiago cheese
1 large Avocado, small diced
1 Tablespoon Fresh Parsley, chopped

Method: Using a vegetable peeler shave long strips of cheese from the top to the bottom end. Continue making ribbons until there are 8 to 12 strips.

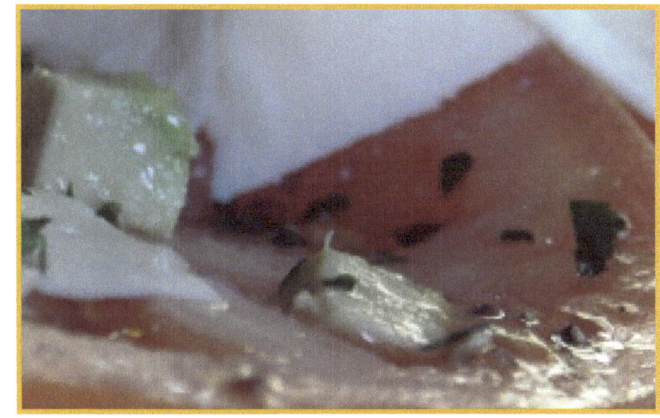

The Finish

On each individual serving plate, layer 4 to 6 slices of tomatoes. Top off with about a teaspoon of avocado on each plate. Drizzle with a little olive oil and check for seasoning. Garnish with cheese and parsley. Serve cool or at room temperature.

HINTS AND TIPS: WORKS GREAT FOR THE SUMMER MONTHS. MOST TIME SALT AND PEPPER IS ALL YOU NEED

SMALL PLATES - SEAFOOD

Seared Ahi Tuna with Passion Vinaigrette

A very simple hearty and elegant dish packed with lots of nutrients. With just a small amount of seasoning Ahi tuna steaks are a great addition to any meal. Serve as an appetizer or small plate. **Wine pairing: Sauvignon Blanc, Chardonnay or Sake**

SEARED AHI TUNA WITH PASSION VINAIGRETTE

Serve: 4　　　　Prep time: 10 Minutes　　　　Cook time: 10 Minutes

Ingredients

2 pounds center cut Ahi tuna steaks
1/2 teaspoon Kosher Salt
Pinch of Cayenne Pepper
1/2 teaspoon Freshly Ground Black Pepper
1 Tablespoon butter, unsalted (Substitute olive oil)
1 Clove Garlic, minced

Method: Slice the tuna fillet into 4 equal size rectangular steaks. Season with salt and cayenne; Lay the tuna steaks out onto a plate, and sprinkle with black pepper evenly on all sides.

In a medium skillet over medium high heat, melt butter, and add the garlic. Carefully place the seasoned tuna in the skillet and sear on all 4 sides to desired doneness about 1 to 2 minutes for rare. Remove steaks from the pan and set aside on a clean cutting board for about 2 to 3 minutes. Meanwhile, make the vinaigrette.

Using a sharp knife, slice the tuna about 1/4 inch thick and serve.

Passion Vinaigrette

1/2 large Shallot, finely chopped
1 Tablespoon Orange Blossom Honey
1 teaspoon Red Pepper Flakes
1/2 Cup Passion Fruit Puree
1/2 teaspoon Kosher Salt
1/2 Cup Extra Virgin Olive Oil

Method: In a food processor or blender combine the first "Five" ingredients. Blend until smooth.

With the machine running, slowly add the oil in a steady stream. Taste and adjust the seasoning.

Garnish

1 Tablespoon Fresh Parsley, minced
1 Tablespoon Fresh Scallions Green part, shaved

Method: Combine ingredients and mix thoroughly.

The Finish

On a serving plate, layer 5 to 6 slices on each plate. Drizzle with a teaspoon of vinaigrette and garnish with herb mixture.

HINTS AND TIPS: FOR A MORE CRUSTED TUNA AND TASTE, USE WHOLE PEPPERCORNS WHEN MELTING THE BUTTER JUST BEFORE ADDING THE TUNA STEAKS

SMALL PLATES – SEAFOOD

Seafood Paella

Full of flavor, color, and texture this dish is a modified version of the traditional Spanish dish, which complements any seasonal menu. The crust is the best.
Wine pairing: Sauvignon Blanc, Syrah, Pinot Noir

SEAFOOD PAELLA

Serve: 4   Prep time: 30 Minutes   Cook time: 40 Minutes

Ingredients

1 Cup of Olive Oil
1/2 Cup Yellow Onions, small diced
4 Cloves Garlic, chopped
1/2 Cup Green Peppers, small diced
1/2 Cup Red Peppers, small diced
1 each Celery stalk, small diced
1 Cup Arborio or Calasparra Rice, uncooked
1/4 teaspoon Saffron
1 Cup White Wine
3 Cups Chicken or Vegetable stock

1 pound Clams, uncooked
1 pound Mussels, uncooked
1 pound Scallops, uncooked
2 Cups Green Peas
1 teaspoon Kosher Salt
1 teaspoon Freshly Ground Black Pepper

Optional

1 pound Shrimp, peeled and de-veined
1/2 pound Crab meat, uncooked

Method: In a large Paella or Sauté pan, heat the oil over medium low heat. Add the onions, garlic, peppers and celery. Sweat mixture for 2 minutes until garlic is translucent.

Add the rice, stirring until evenly coated. Add the saffron and wine; Stir occasionally; Let the rice absorb the liquid about 5 minutes. Then add a 1/3 of the stock just enough to cover the rice. Bring to a simmer and cook for 10 minutes or until liquid is fully absorbed.

After the stock is soaked in for the second time, add the final stock, the clams, mussels, scallops and peas. (Optional ingredients may be added at this point). Taste and adjust seasoning. Cover paella and lower heat. Let simmer for 7 to 10 minutes. Check for seasoning. Remove from the heat and serve immediately.

The Finish

Transfer 3 ounces (about 2 spoons) of rice to each individual plate. Top off with an even distribution of seafood. Serve warm.

> **HINTS AND TIPS:** PAELLA IS A GREAT DISH FOR LARGE GATHERINGS OR FAMILY STYLE. YOU CAN SERVE DIRECTLY FROM THE PAN OR INDIVIDUAL PLATES

SMALL PLATES – MEATS

Pan-Seared Sliced Beef with Green Beans

Very reliable dish for any occasion with leftover meat like steak and beef rounds. The green beans and tortilla chips adds a fresh and texture balance.
Wine pairing: Merlot or Bordeaux or Margaritas

PAN-SEARED SLICED BEEF WITH GREEN BEANS

Serve: 4　　　　　　　　　Prep time: 10 Minutes　　　　　　　Cook time: 15 Minutes

Ingredients

2 Tablespoons Canola Oil
2 pounds Rib eye or (sirloin, flank steak, round)
1/2 teaspoon Freshly Ground Pepper
1/2 teaspoon Kosher Salt

Method: Season the steak with salt and pepper. In a large skillet or sauté pan, heat the oil over medium high heat.

Transfer the steak to the pan and sear on all sides for about 3 to 5 minutes for medium rare. Remove from the pan, and let rest for 2 to 4 minutes before slicing. Slice 1/4 to 1/2 inch thick and serve warm.

Tortilla Chips

3 each Tortilla　　　　　　　Pinch of Cayenne
Olive Oil　　　　　　　　　　Pinch of Paprika
Kosher Salt

Green Beans

1 Tablespoon Kosher Salt
1 pound Green Beans, trimmed
1 Tablespoon of butter

Method: Bring a 2 quart pot water to a boil. Add salt and stir. Once salt is dissolved add the beans. Reduce heat to medium. Cover and cook for about 4 to 5 minutes until beans are crisp tender to the bite.

Remove from the heat, strain and drain. While still warm, combine the beans and butter in a medium bowl; toss until well coated. Season to taste.

Method: Preheat oven to 250°F (121°C). Brush tortilla with oil and season with spices. Cut in halves, then halves again two more time. Place on baking sheet in a single layer. Bake for 15 minutes or until edges are lightly brown.

The Finish

On warm plates, layer 5 to 6 slices of beef on each plate. Evenly divide the green beans and tortilla chips.

HINTS AND TIPS: BROWNING MEATS HELP SEAL IN THEIR JUICES. IF YOU PREFER A MUCH MORE COOKED MEAT, LET IT SIT IN THE PAN FOR ANOTHER 3 TO 5 MINUTES.

SMALL PLATES – MEATS

Bacon, Capers, Braised Green Flat Bread

This flat bread recipe is just as impressive topped with other meats. Very similar to a pizza recipe is great for sport gatherings or next day leftovers.
Beer pairing: Lager or Dark Stout

BACON, CAPERS, BRAISED GREEN FLAT BREAD

Serve: 4   Prep time: 10 Minutes   Cook time: 25 Minutes

Ingredients

4 Pita Bread or Pita Pockets
1 Cup Mornay Sauce (recipe included)
2 Cups Braised Greens, chopped (recipe included)
1 Cup Pickled Red Onion (Recipe page 78)
3 Strips of Bacon, finely chopped
1 Cup Caramelized Onions (Recipe page 77)
1 Tablespoon Capers, drained and chopped
1 Cup Gruyere, grated

Method: Preheat the oven to 375°F (190°C). On a clean flat working surface or using a baking sheet, place pitas flat side down. Spread a layer of the Mornay sauce from center of pita coming out about 1/4 inch from the edges.

Top off evenly with greens, pickled onions, bacon, caramelized onions and capers. Finish with a layer of Gruyere.

Transfer to the oven and bake for 7 to 10 minutes until cheese is fully melted and lightly browned on top. Remove from oven and slice into fourths.

The Finish

On a warm plate serve 4 slices per guest. This equals one flat bread per guest. Serve warm.

Braised Greens

1/2 Cup Olive Oil
2 each Cloves Garlic, minced
1/2 pound Kale
1/2 pound Mustard Greens
1 teaspoon Red Pepper Flakes
1 Cup Water
Pinch of Salt

Method: In a medium pot, heat oil over medium heat. Add garlic for 20 seconds, then add kale, mustard greens, salt and pepper flakes. Add the water and cover. Reduce heat to medium low. Cook for 3 to 5 minutes until greens are starting to wilt - slightly under cook. Do not overcook.

Mornay Sauce

6 ounces Bechamel (Recipe page 77)
1 Cup Gruyere Cheese, grated
Salt and Pepper
2 Cups Milk, warm

Method: In a medium sauce pan over low heat, add the bechamel and stir. Add cheese and seasoning; Continue to stir. Turn off the heat and adjust consistency with milk. Consistency should be cheesy.

HINTS AND TIPS: INSTEAD OF MAKING A ROUX TO CREATE CLASSIC BECHAMEL USE A CREAM REDUCTION WITH STOCK FOR A MORE MODERN TECHNIQUE

MAIN DISHES

MEATS AND POULTRY

PASSION GLAZED PORK BELLY WITH CHIVE GNOCCHI

TANDOORI CHICKEN WITH BASMATI RICE

BRAISED LAMB WITH ISRAELI COUSCOUS

VEGETARIAN

STUFFED MUSHROOM EGGPLANT CAPS

OPEN-FACED TOMATO PEA PESTO SANDWICH

SEAFOOD

PAN-SEARED TROUT WITH HORSERADISH RISOTTO

CRISPY SKIN SALMON WITH ROASTED ASPARAGUS SALAD

MAIN DISHES – MEATS AND POULTRY

Passion Glazed Pork Belly with Chive Gnocchi

This melt in your mouth favorite is always a crowd pleaser, especially when paired with baby carrots and chives. Pork belly is very popular among Asian cuisine.
Wine pairing: Malbec, Merlot, Brandy

PASSION GLAZED PORK BELLY WITH CHIVE GNOCCHI

Serve: 4　　　　　Prep time: 30 Minutes　　　　　Cook time: 45 Minutes

Ingredients

1 pound Pork Belly, cut into small squares (2 in x 2 in)
2 Tablespoons Canola Oil
1 large Yellow Onion, Chopped
2 Cloves Garlic, Chopped
2 medium Carrots, Chopped
2 Tablespoons Soy Sauce
2 Cups Chicken or Beef Stock
Sprig of Thyme
1/2 teaspoon Whole Peppercorn
2 Bay leaves
1 Cup Passion Fruit Puree
8 Baby Carrots, halved
Chives Gnocchi (Recipe page 78)

Method: Allow pork belly to sit at room temperature for 10 minutes. Pat dry the pork belly with kitchen paper and score the skin with a sharp knife. In a large skillet, heat the oil over medium-high heat. Place the pork belly skin side down and then sear on all sides for about 30 seconds. Remove pork belly from the pan and set aside.

Add the onion, garlic, carrots and cook for 2 minutes. Return pork belly to the pot and add the soy sauce, stock, thyme, peppercorn and bay leaves. Cover and bring to a boil. Reduce to a simmer and cook for 30 to 35 minutes. While the pork belly is braising prepare the Chive Gnocchi.

Pork belly is ready when soft and tender. Heat the puree until it reaches a syrup like consistency. Brush or pour the puree over the skin of the pork belly. Cover and continue to cook for another 10 minutes. Remove pork belly from pot and keep warm. Bring the pot to a boil and reduce the liquid to about 2 cups to make a Demi reduction. Remove from the heat.

Bring a small pot of water to a boil. Add the baby carrots, cook for 2 minutes. Remove from heat.

The Finish

In a warm serving bowl, pour about a Tablespoon of sauce into each dish. Place about 4 to 6 Gnocchi's as the base. Top off with a square of pork belly. Add the baby carrots and garnish with chives. Serve warm.

HINTS AND TIPS: PORK BELLY IS A VERY FATTY, BONELESS AND SCRUMPTIOUS CUT OF MEAT TRY TO KEEP PORTION SIZE SMALL

MAIN DISHES – MEATS AND POULTRY

Tandoori Chicken with Basmati Rice

A staple dish from India that includes a variety of yellow and red colors. Tandoori spice compliments the chicken served with lime, aromatic and soft rice.
Wine pairing: Cabernet Sauvignon, Syrah, Chardonnay

TANDOORI CHICKEN WITH BASMATI RICE

Serve: 4   Prep time: 90 Minutes   Cook time: 50 Minutes

Ingredients

- 1 1/2 pound Chicken legs, skinned, slashed
- 2 teaspoons Paprika
- 2 teaspoons Sea Salt flakes
- 1 Cup Plain Yogurt
- 2 teaspoons hot Red Chili Powder
- 1 teaspoon Fresh Ginger, grated
- 2 each Cloves Garlic, crushed
- 1 teaspoon Cumin Seeds, crushed
- 1 each Cinnamon Stick, crushed
- 1 Cup unsalted Butter, melted

Method: Dry the chicken well with kitchen towel and rub the paprika and salt into the slashes and surfaces. In a large bowl mix the yogurt, chili, ginger and garlic. Using an electric spice grinder, grind the cumin, cinnamon to a powder. Add to the yogurt marinade. Dip the chicken into the marinade until well coated, and then chill for 1 hour or overnight. When ready to cook, preheat a heavy baking sheet at 400°F (204°C) for 10 minutes. Brush it with butter and heat until melted. Add the chicken and drizzle with remaining butter. Cook in the upper third of the oven for 30 to 40 minutes. Check for doneness by piercing the chicken with a point of a sharp knife, the juices should run clear yellow. If not, cook a little longer then serve.

Basmati Rice

- 1 Cup Basmati Rice
- 2 Tablespoons Vegetable Oil
- 1/2 teaspoon Whole Cumin Seeds
- Kosher salt
- 2 Cups Water

Method: Rinse the rice 3 to 4 times with water. Drain and set aside. In a deep pan, heat the vegetable oil over medium high heat. Add the cumin seeds and cook until they sizzle. Add the rice and salt; Stir. Add the water and bring to a boil. Reduce the heat to low. Cover with lid and cook for about 15 to 20 minutes or until most of the water has evaporated. Remove from the heat and let sit for 5 minutes. Fluff using fork before serving.

The Finish

On a warm plate, serve 4 ounces of rice, topped with chicken and garnish with lime and red onion.

HINTS AND TIPS: GREAT WAY TO KNOW WHEN LIQUID EVAPORATES FROM RICE, LOOK FOR CRATERS

MAIN DISHES – MEATS AND POULTRY

Braised Lamb with Israeli Couscous

A stunning main course for any occasion, this braised lamb served with Israeli couscous will have guest talking at your next gathering. It's real easy to put together.
Wine pairing: Merlot, Sauvignon Blanc, Cabernet Sauvignon

BRAISED LAMB WITH ISRAELI COUSCOUS

Serve: 4   Prep time: 15 Minutes   Cook time: 90 Minutes

Ingredients

- 2 1/2 pounds Boneless Leg of Lamb, trimmed
- 1 teaspoon Kosher Salt and Pepper
- 1/4 Cup Canola Oil
- 2 each Yellow Onions, chopped
- 3 Celery Stalks, chopped
- 3 medium Carrots, peeled, chopped
- 2 Cups Red Wine
- 6 Cups Water
- 2 Sprigs Thyme
- 1 Sprig Rosemary
- 2 Cloves Garlic, crushed

Method: Preheat oven to 350°F (177°C). Season the lamb generously with salt and pepper. Heat the oil in a large ovenproof pot over high heat. Sear lamb on all sides but do not scorch. Transfer lamb to a platter. Add onions, celery and carrots to the pot. Reduce heat to medium low and cook until onions begin to caramelize about 3 minutes. Add the red wine followed by 4 cups water. Bring to a boil. Return lamb and its juices to the pot. Add remaining water just enough to cover lamb depending on the size of pot. Add thyme, rosemary and garlic. Bring to a simmer, cover with lid and transfer to oven.

Lamb is ready if it can easily pull apart when pierce with a fork, about 1 1/2 hours. Transfer lamb to a platter and strain stock through a sieve over a large bowl. Discard solids and reduce heat to a simmer. Cook until liquid reduces to 3 cups about 15 minutes. Meanwhile, prepare the Couscous. Remove pot from the heat.

Israeli Couscous

- 2 Cups Israeli Couscous
- 1 Tablespoon Butter, unsalted
- 2 Cups Lamb or vegetable Stock
- 1/2 teaspoon Kosher Salt
- 1/4 teaspoon Freshly Ground Pepper

Method: Preheat oven to 250°F (112°C). On a baking sheet, spread the Couscous out in single layer and toast for about 3 to 5 minutes until lightly browned. Remove from the oven and allow to cool. In a medium pot, melt butter, add the couscous and stock. Simmer for 12 minutes or until the liquid has evaporated. Remove the couscous from the heat. Season to taste with salt and pepper.

The Finish

In warm serving bowls or plates, serve 3 to 4 ounces of Couscous, portion lamb evenly among dishes and garnish with chopped herbs.

HINTS AND TIPS: RESERVE ABOUT 1 TO 2 CUPS OF BRAISING LIQUID FOR COUSCOUS AND LATER USE

MAIN DISHES – VEGETARIAN

Stuffed Mushroom Eggplant Caps

A subtle blend of eggplant, tomatoes and root vegetables, topped with Parmesan cheese stuffed into a Portobello mushroom and baked to perfection.
Wine pairing: Pinot Noir, Zinfandel

STUFFED MUSHROOM EGGPLANT CAPS

Serve: 4   Prep time: 10 Minutes   Cook time: 15 Minutes

Filling

4 Portobello Mushroom Caps, trimmed
2 Tablespoons Olive Oil
2 Cloves Garlic, chopped
2 Tablespoons Red Peppers, medium diced
2 Tablespoons Green Peppers, medium diced
1 large Eggplant, medium diced

2 Roma Tomatoes, medium diced
Kosher Salt
Fresh Ground Black Pepper
1 Cup Quinoa, cooked (Recipe page 78)

Method: Preheat oven to 300°F (148°C). Line a baking sheet with a silpat or cooking spray. Under cold running water, gently clean mushrooms thoroughly then Pat dry.

In a large sauté pan over medium heat add garlic, peppers and eggplant. Sauté for 30 seconds until eggplant is evenly coated. Season with a pinch of salt and pepper, reduce heat to medium low. Add the tomatoes, and drizzle with olive oil. Remove mixture from heat and add quinoa. Stir thoroughly.

Arrange the mushroom caps onto the baking sheet. Using a spoon, fill each Mushroom cap with 3 ounces (about two spoons) of filling. Transfer to oven and bake for 10 minutes or until vegetables are starting to brown. Remove from the oven.

Garnish

2 Tablespoons Parmesan, grated
1 Tablespoon Chopped Herbs (Parsley, Dill, Rosemary, Thyme)

The Finish

Transfer caps to serving plates. Drizzle with olive oil and garnish with Parmesan and herbs.

HINTS AND TIPS: GREAT DISH FOR GRILLING. SUPER EASY AND QUICK TO PREPARE

MAIN DISHES – VEGETARIAN

Open-Faced Tomato Pea Pesto Sandwich

Perfect for summer this refreshing pea pesto and tomato sandwich will brighten your lunch and spring forward your day. **Wine pairing: Chardonnay or Riesling.**

OPEN-FACED TOMATO PEA PESTO SANDWICH

Serve: 4   Prep time: 15 Minutes   Cook time: 5 Minutes

Topping

1 large tomato, sliced 1/2 inch thick
1 Tablespoon Fresh Parsley or Basil, minced

Pea Pesto

2 Cup English Peas
1 Clove Garlic, minced
1/2 Cup Parmesan Cheese, grated
1 teaspoon Kosher Salt
1/2 teaspoon Freshly Ground Black Pepper
1/2 Cup Olive Oil

Method: Pulse together in a food processor the peas, garlic, Parmesan, salt and pepper.

With the machine running, slowly add oil and mix until well combined, about 1 to 2 minutes. Check for seasoning. Transfer to a small bowl and set aside.

Base

1 Baguette or French Bread cut into halved then thirds
1 Tablespoon Olive Oil

Method: Preheat oven to 350°F (176°C). On a large baking sheet arrange bread slices in a single layer with cut side up. Drizzle with olive oil and toast in oven for 2 to 3 minutes or until lightly golden brown. Remove from oven and serve warm.

Alternative using a Grill:

Preheat grill, brush the cut side of the bread with olive oil. Once grill is hot, place bread cut side down on grill and toast for 2 to 3 minutes. Remove from grill and serve warm.

The Finish

On a serving plate, place two slices of bread. Spread about 1 Tablespoon of Pesto on each slice. Top off with two slices of tomatoes. Season to taste with salt and pepper. Garnish with the herbs and serve immediately.

HINTS AND TIPS: INSTEAD OF USING A GRILL ANY DRY HEATING METHOD CAN BE USED LIKE AN OVEN OR BROILER.

MAIN DISHES – SEAFOOD

Pan-Seared Trout with Horseradish Risotto

Get ready for a tasty weeknight meal or impressive dinner party taking only a few minutes to prepare. Elegant and full of flavor with the risotto adding a nice balance of spiciness from the mild horseradish flavor. **Wine pairing: Chardonnay, Sake or Pinot Grigio**

PAN-SEARED TROUT WITH HORSERADISH RISOTTO

Serve: 4　　　　　　　　　　Prep time: 15 Minutes　　　　　　　　Cook time: 30 Minutes

Ingredients

4 each Trout fillets
4 Tablespoons Olive Oil
1 teaspoon Kosher Salt
1/2 teaspoon Freshly Ground Black Pepper
1/2 Cup White Wine
2 Tablespoon Butter, unsalted
Capers and Scallions for Garnish

Method: Rub fillets with oil, and season with salt and pepper. Allow to marinate at room temperature for 10 minutes. Preheat a heavy skillet on high heat and add oil. Pat dry fillets. Add 2 pieces at a time to the pan, skin side down, Cook about 2 to 3 minutes until skin is slightly crisp. Flip to the other side and cook for 1 to 2 minute. Remove fish from pan. To make the butter sauce, deglaze pan with white wine and add 4 Tablespoons of butter. Add capers and stir vigorously over medium heat.

Horseradish Risotto

2 Tablespoons Olive Oil
1 Clove Garlic, minced
2 Cups Arborio Rice
1/4 Cup White Wine
3 Cups Fish or Vegetable Stock
2 Cups Parmesan Cheese, grated
2 Tablespoons plain (prepared) horseradish, steeped in 1 Cup heavy cream
Salt and Pepper to Taste

Method: Heat the oil on medium low heat, then add the garlic, cooked for 20 seconds. Add the rice and stir until all the rice is evenly coated. Add the white wine and simmer for 1 minute until liquid evaporates about 3 to 5 minutes.

Add the stock, just enough to cover the rice. Cook for 10 minutes. Once liquid is absorbed add another ladle of stock. Cook for another 10 minutes until liquid is absorbed once more. Add the cream and stir thoroughly making sure rice is well coated. Finally, add the Parmesan cheese and mix well. Remove from the heat.

The Finish

On a serving plate, place about 3 to 4 ounces of rice on each plate. Top off with the Trout fillet and pour about 1 Tablespoon of butter sauce over the top.

HINTS AND TIPS: IF THE RISOTTO IS DRYING OUT, ADD A LITTLE MORE STOCK. MAKE SURE THE PAN IS HOT WHEN COOKING FISH

MAIN DISHES – SEAFOOD

Crispy Skin Salmon with Roasted Asparagus Salad

You don't have to be living near water to get the best of this dish. Absolute incredible natural colors and flavor.
Wine pairing: Chardonnay or Zinfandel

CRISPY SKIN SALMON WITH ROASTED ASPARAGUS SALAD

Serve: 4   Prep time: 15 Minutes   Cook time: 20 Minutes

Crispy Skin Salmon

4 each (6 ounce) center-cut Salmon fillets with skin
2 Tablespoons Olive Oil
Salt and Pepper to Taste

1/2 Cup White Wine
4 Tablespoons Butter, unsalted

Method: Scale and wash the salmon under cold running water and pat dry. Using a sharp knife cut small slits in the salmon skin. This will prevent the skin from curling. Put a little salt and pepper, and olive oil inside the cuts. Don't over season. Set aside for 10 minutes.

Preheat a skillet on medium high heat. Add oil. Once the pan is hot and starts to sizzle, place salmon fillets [Skin side down] and cook until the skin is crispy about 2 to 3 minutes. When the salmon has changed to a lighter pink, flip to the other side using a fish spatula. Cook the other side for about 2 to 4 minutes. Remove fillets from pan. To make the butter sauce, deglaze pan with white wine and add 4 Tablespoons of butter. Season with salt and stir vigorously over medium low heat.

Roasted Asparagus Salad

1 bunch Green Asparagus, trimmed
4 Tablespoons olive oil

Kosher Salt and Black Pepper
1 head Romaine, washed, dry, chopped

Method: Preheat oven to 425°F (225°C). Lay the asparagus in a single layer with a double layer of heavy-duty aluminum foil. Drizzle with the olive oil and toss to coat. Fold the edges of the foil to make a tray. Roast in the oven for about 5 minutes. Gently toss the spears with tongs and roast just until tender and asparagus tips begin to brown. Transfer to a serving plate. Meanwhile, in a small bowl gently toss the chopped romaine with oil and season with salt and pepper. Serve.

The Finish

Arrange asparagus spears on each plate and top off with a bed of romaine. Top each plate with a salmon fillet skin side up. Pour a Tablespoon of butter sauce over the salmon.

HINTS AND TIPS: IT'S ALWAYS GOOD TO WASH AND SPIN DRY YOUR LEAFY GREENS BEFORE USE

DESSERTS

SWEETS

PASSION FRUIT SOUFFLE
WITH PEAR PASSION SAUCE

CARDAMOM ICE CREAM WITH
DANISH BUTTER COOKIE

CRÈME BRULEE CHOCOLATE
MOUSSE

REFRESHER

MOJITO SORBET

DESSERTS

Passion Fruit Soufflé with Pear Passion Sauce

Lightly baked cake made with egg yolks and beaten egg whites combined with passion fruit served as sweetened dessert with a delectable pear passion sauce.
Wine pairing: Muscat, Brandy or Coffee

PASSION FRUIT SOUFFLE WITH PEAR PASSION SAUCE

Serve: 4   Prep time: 15 Minutes   Cook time: 20 Minutes

Ingredients

4 Tablespoons Butter, unsalted
4 large Egg yolks, at room temperature
2 1/4 fluid ounces Passion Fruit Puree

4 large Egg whites, at room temperature
1 1/4 ounce sugar
2 ounces icing sugar, for dusting

Method: Preheat the oven to 350°F (177°C). Butter the inside and rims of each (6 ounce) ramekin or soufflé dishes. Dust with sugar. Tap out the excess sugar and put the dishes on a baking tray. To make the soufflé, whisk together the egg yolks and passion fruit puree in a bowl, and set aside. Whisk the egg whites on medium-low speed just until foamy. Increase the speed to medium-high and gradually add the sugar, beating until the whites form glossy medium-stiff peaks.

Using a spatula, gently fold the meringue - "egg whites" into the yolk mixture in three additions until well incorporated. Using a piping bag or spoon, fill the dishes up to their rims. Run your thumb along the outside edge of the dishes to remove any excess butter and sugar. Bake the soufflés for 15 to 20 minutes, until puffed and lightly golden. If you touch the top, they should be firm with center still a bit wobbly.

Pear Passion Sauce

1 Tablespoon unsalted butter
4 1/2 ounce sugar

1 medium Pear, small diced
1 Cup Passion Fruit Puree

Method: In a small sauce pan, melt the butter then add the sugar, a few tablespoons at a time, stirring after each addition, until it melts, and cook until the syrup turns a light golden brown. Add the diced pear and continue to cook, while stirring, until they are tender and caramelized about 10 minutes. Stir in the passion fruit puree and heat for 1 to 2 minutes. Remove from the heat and keep warm.

The Finish

Dust soufflés with icing sugar and gently cut in the middle pouring a Tablespoon of sauce. Serve Immediately.

HINTS AND TIPS: SOUFFLÉS CAN BE INTIMIDATING. KEY POINTS TO REMEMBER ARE PREPARATION AND TEMPERATURE.

DESSERTS – SWEETS

Cardamom Ice Cream with Danish Butter Cookie

Cardamom has a very strong and bold flavor but when paired with a Danish butter cookie it's just delicious.
Drink pairing: Coffee or Cappuccino

CARDAMOM ICE CREAM WITH DANISH BUTTER COOKIE

Serve 4   Prep time: 15 Minutes   Cook time: 20 Minutes

Cardamom Ice Cream

2 Cups milk or light cream
1 Vanilla bean, split lengthwise
8 Whole Green Cardamom pods, lightly crushed
4 Egg yolks
3/4 Cup Sugar
3/4 cup Heavy Whipping Cream
1/8 teaspoon Ground Cardamom

Method: In a heavy sauce pan, add the milk, or light cream, vanilla bean and crushed cardamom pods. Bring to a simmer, cover and let infuse for 7 minutes. Remove from heat. Take out the vanilla bean and scrape seeds into the liquid. Remove the crushed green cardamom pods. Beat the egg yolks and sugar until thick and pale. Gently reheat the milk or cream and beat a little into the egg yolks. Pour the egg mixture into the cream and return the pan to low heat. Stir until the custard is thick enough to coat the back of a spoon; it will take several minutes. Do not boil. Remove the pan from the heat and continue to stir until mixture is almost cooled. Whip the cream lightly and fold it into the custard. Add the ground cardamom. Transfer to an Ice cream maker and freeze.

Danish Butter Cookie

1 Cup sweet Butter or unsalted butter
1 Cup Sugar
1 Large Egg
1 teaspoon Vanilla
1 Cup Flour, sifted
1/4 teaspoon Salt

Method: Preheat oven to 400°F (204°C). In a large bowl, cream together the butter and sugar until light and fluffy. Beat in the egg, and then stir in the vanilla. Combine the flour and salt; stir into the sugar mixture. Cover dough, and chill for at least one hour. Chill cookie sheet. Press dough out onto ungreased, chilled cookie sheet. Bake for 8 to 10 minutes until lightly golden around the edges. Remove from oven, cool slightly.

The Finish

Divide cookies evenly amongst guest and top off with a scope of ice cream. Serve immediately.

HINTS AND TIPS: CARDAMOM IS VERY STRONG SPICE, USE CAUTION WHEN USING IN ANY RECIPE

DESSERTS – CRÈME BRULEE CHOCOLATE MOUSSE

Serve: 4　　　　　　　　　　　Prep time: 3 Hours　　　　　　　　　　Cook time: 20 Minutes

Crème Brulee

2/3 Cup Whipping Cream
1/3 Cup Whole Milk
1/2 teaspoon flavored powdered Gelatin

1/2 Vanilla Bean, Split Lengthwise
4 Large Egg yolks
1/4 Cup Sugar
1/3 Cup Mascarpone Cheese

Method: In a medium sauce pan, add the cream and milk. Sprinkle the gelatin over the cream mixture and set aside for 5 minutes to allow the gelatin to soften. Scrape the seeds from the vanilla bean into the cream mixture.

Bring to a simmer over medium-low heat, stirring until the gelatin dissolves, about 10 minutes. In a separate medium bowl, whisk the yolks and sugar to blend. Whisk in the mascarpone and gradually whisk in the hot cream mixture. Transfer the mixture to the same saucepan. Stir constantly over medium-low heat for 6 minutes, or until the foam subsides and the custard thickens enough to coat a spoon. Transfer the custard to a clean bowl and set the bowl over a large bowl of ice water. Stir the custard until it is cold but not set; discard the vanilla bean. Set the custard aside. Reserve the bowl of ice water.

Chocolate Mousse

5 ounces Dark bittersweet chocolate, chopped
2 Large Eggs

1/2 Cup Sugar
2 Cups Heavy Cream

Stir the chocolate in a heatproof bowl set over a saucepan of hot water until melted. Using an electric mixer on medium-high speed beat the eggs and sugar in a large bowl until medium peaks form, about 8 minutes. Whisk in the chocolate mixture then set the bowl over ice water. Whisk the cream in a medium bowl until very thick. Fold about 1/2 cup of the cream into the chocolate mixture to help lighten it. Continue whisking the remaining cream until soft peaks begin to form. Gently fold the whipped cream into the chocolate mixture.

To Finish

Spoon half of the chocolate mousse into each of the wine glasses. Refrigerate the mousse in the glasses for 15 minutes. Then pour the custard over the mousse in the glasses. Refrigerate for another 30 minutes, or until the custard is set. Spoon the remaining mousse over the custard. Refrigerate for 1 hour before serving.

REFRESHER – MOJITO SORBET

Serve: 10 Prep time: 10 Minutes Cook time: 5 Minutes

Ingredients

1/4 Cup Water
1/4 Cup White sugar
2 Tablespoons Mint leaves, packed
1 Tablespoon Lime zest, grated
1/4 cup Freshly squeezed lime juice
1/4 cup Sparkling Water
1 1/2 teaspoons Malibu Coconut rum

Method: Heat the water, sugar, and mint leaves in a saucepan over medium heat, and stir until the sugar is dissolved. Bring the mixture to a boil, reduce heat, and simmer for 3 to 5 minutes to extract the mint flavor. Set the mixture aside to cool, and strain out the mint leaves.

Pour the cooled mint mixture, lime zest, lime juice, sparkling water, and rum into a bowl and mix well.

The Finish

Pour into the container of an ice cream maker, and freeze according to the manufacturer's instructions. Serve immediately for a softer texture, or freeze in a sealed container for a harder sorbet. Let hard-frozen sorbet thaw a few minutes before serving.

Sub Recipes

- **White Chicken Stock**
- **White Vegetable Stock**
- **Brine Recipe**
- **Additional Sub Recipes**
- Bechamel Sauce
- Caramelized Onions
- Candied Pecans
- Creme fraiche
- Pickled onions
- Quinoa

WHITE CHICKEN STOCK

Makes: 1 Gallon   Prep time: 15 Minutes   Cook time: 50 Minutes

Ingredients

7 pounds Chicken Bones
1 1/2 Gallons Cold Water
1/2 pound Yellow Onions, medium diced
1/4 pound Carrot; medium diced
1/4 pound Celery, medium diced
3 each Whole Peppercorn, crushed
2 Bay leaves
Sprig of Thyme
3 Cloves Garlic, crushed

Method: Rinse bones in cold water to remove blood and impurities. Place bones in stock pot and cover with cold water. Bring to a boil, and then reduce to a simmer. Skim off the scum as it appears on the surface. Simmer for 25 to 30 minutes.

Add the onions, carrots, celery, peppercorn, bay leaves, thyme and garlic. If preferred, wrap the peppercorn, bay leaves, garlic and thyme in a cheesecloth to make a sachet before adding to the pot. Simmer for 20 minutes.

The Finish

Taste for flavor and balance. Strain, and allow to cool before properly storing.

HINT AND TIPS: STORE IN SMALL PORTIONS FOR LATER USE

WHITE VEGETABLE STOCK

Makes: 1 Gallon   Prep time: 15 Minutes   Cook time: 30 Minutes

Ingredients

2 Tablespoons Olive Oil
1 pound Yellow Onion, medium diced
1/2 pound Carrots, medium diced
1/2 pound Fennel; medium diced
1/4 pound Leeks, halve lengthwise, diced
1/4 pound Celery, medium diced
5 Cloves Garlic, crushed
1 1/2 Gallons Water, cold
2 Bay leaves
Sprig of thyme
3 each Whole Peppercorn, crushed

Method: Heat oil and add onion, carrots and fennel; sweat until soft about 4 minutes. Add the leeks, celery and garlic; sweat until softened about 3 minutes.

Add water and bay leaves, thyme and peppercorn. Bring to a simmer. Cook for 15 to 25 minutes.

The Finish

Taste for flavor and balance. Strain, and cool before properly storing.

HINT AND TIPS: STORE IN SMALL PORTIONS FOR LATER USE

BRINE RECIPE

Makes: 1 Gallon   Prep time: 5 Minutes   Cook time: 10 Minutes

Brining is a great way to add flavor and retain moisture. When you add your poultry to the brine solution the liquid should be icy. The first step in the process is selecting your brining ingredients. Beyond the standard list, we've added other ingredients to help provide additional flavors.

Brine Ingredients

1 1/2 gallon Water
3 Bay leaves
3 1/2 Cups Sugar
2 Tablespoons Fresh peppercorns, crushed
3 Cups Kosher Salt
4 Cloves garlic, peeled and smashed
2 Sprigs Thyme
2 teaspoon Allspice berries

Method: Remove any giblets. Rinse the bird inside and out. Be sure to rinse under cold running water, this will guarantee you don't start cooking the bird.

In a large stainless steel pan, prepare your brine by combining all ingredients. Bring to a boil; stir ingredients until all of the salt and sugar is dissolved. Remove from heat, and allow brine to cool. Add 2 quarts of ice during this stage.

Transfer bird to a large container or brining bag. Be sure the container will fit in your fridge or cooler. Add brine, covering the entire bird. Place in the refrigerator or cooler for at least 2 hours depending on the size of bird.

HINT AND TIPS: BRINE SOLUTION SHOULD BE ICY - COLD. ROOM TEMPERATURE BRINE MAY CAUSE SERIOUS ILLNESS

ADDITIONAL SUB RECIPES

Caramelized onions

(Makes 2 Cups)

3 Tablespoons Butter, unsalted
Pinch of Sugar
2 large Onions, thinly sliced
Salt and Pepper

Method: Melt butter in large skillet over medium heat. Add onions and toss to coat with butter. Cover and slowly cook onions, stirring occasionally, for 5 minutes or until a golden color is reached.

Turn heat up to medium high and begin to brown the onions, stirring constantly about 10 more minutes. Check and adjust for seasoning.

Bechamel

(Makes 2 Cups)

2 Tablespoon Butter, unsalted
1 Tablespoon all-purpose flour
2 Cups Milk
1 teaspoon Kosher Salt
1/2 teaspoon Fresh grated nutmeg

Method: In a medium saucepan, heat the butter over medium-low heat until melted. Add flour and stir until smooth. Cook about 3 to 5 minutes light brown. Meanwhile, heat the milk in a separate pan until just about to boil. Add the hot milk to the butter mixture 1 cup at a time, whisking continuously until very smooth. Cook for 7 minutes, stirring constantly, then remove from heat. Season with salt and nutmeg.

Creme Fraiche

(Makes 1 Cup)

2 Tablespoons cultured buttermilk
2 Cups heavy cream (pasteurized, not ultra pasteurized or sterilized, and with no additives)

Method: Combine the buttermilk and cream in a saucepan and heat to (not more than 85°F (29°C) on an instant reading thermometer. Pour into a clean glass jar. Partially cover and let stand at room temperature (between 65°F and 75°F) for 8 to 24 hours, or until thickened.

Stir and refrigerate at least 24 hours before using. The cream will keep about 2 weeks in the refrigerator.

Candied Pecans

(Makes 2 Cups)

1 Cup Sugar
1 teaspoon Cinnamon, ground
1 teaspoon Kosher Salt
2 large Egg "whites" and 1 teaspoon of water
1 pound Pecan halves

Method: Preheat oven to 250°F (121°C). Combine sugar, cinnamon, egg mixture and mix in pecans to coat evenly. Arrange on a baking sheet, spread out pecans into a single layer. Bake for 30 to 40 minutes, stirring every 15 minutes until lightly brown. Remove and cool.

ADDITIONAL SUB RECIPES Cont...

Pickled Red Onions

(Makes about 2 Cup)

1 teaspoon Kosher Salt
1/2 Apple Cider Vinegar
1 Tablespoon Sugar
1 Red Onion, thinly sliced

Method: In a small bowl, whisk together first "Three" ingredients until sugar and salt dissolve. Place onion in a jar or bowl and pour vinegar mixture over top of onions.

Let sit at room temperature for 1 hour, then cover and chill. Best when left overnight.

Quinoa

(Makes 3 Cups)

1 Cup Quinoa
2 Cups Water
1 teaspoon Kosher Salt

Method: Rinse quinoa in a fine mesh sieve until water runs clear. Drain and transfer to a medium pot. Add 2 cups water and salt; Bring to a boil.

Cover and reduce heat to medium low and simmer until water is absorbed about 10 to 15 minutes. Set aside off the heat for 5 minutes; uncover and fluff with a fork.

Chive Gnocchi's

(Makes 6 to 8 servings)

1 1/2 pounds Russet Potatoes
1 large Egg yolk, beaten
1 teaspoon coarse kosher salt
1 Cup (or more) All-purpose Flour
Large pinch of freshly grated nutmeg
1 Tablespoon Olive Oil

Method: Fill a 2 quart pot with water. Bring to a boil. Add potatoes and reduce heat to medium; Cover and cook for 15 to 20 minutes or until tender. Cool and Drain, remove skin from potatoes and mash.

Place 2 cups of the mashed potatoes in a large bowl (save any remaining mash for another use). Stir in egg and 1 teaspoon salt. Gradually beat in flour until blended (dough will become firm and elastic). Turn onto a lightly floured surface and knead 15 times. Roll into
1/2 inch wide ropes. Cut ropes into 1-inch pieces. Press down with a lightly floured fork.

Using the same 2 quart pot fill with water and bring to a boil, add salt. Add gnocchi in small batches; cook for 8 to 10 minutes or until gnocchi float to the top and are cooked through. Remove with a slotted spoon.

In a medium sauté pan, melt butter. Add the Gnocchi's and sauté until lightly brown. About 30 to 40 seconds. Serve immediately.

Resources

- **Basic Prep Checklist**
- **Weight Conversions**
- **Liquid Conversions**
- **Temperature Conversions**
- **Quick Cooking Reference**

BASIC PREP CHECKLIST

Recipe:	Date:
Yield:	Serve:
Portion Size:	

Amount	Unit	Ingredients	Equipment	Method

Notes:

WEIGHT CONVERSIONS

Recipes that use the imperial system measure many ingredients by weight instead of volume. This can be confusing especially if you don't own a kitchen scale and you are using measuring cups or spoons. There is a difference between measuring liquid and dry ingredients.

Dry measuring cups are used to measure the volume of bulk solid ingredients such as salt, sugars and flours. They usually come in a set, typically of 1/4, 1/3, 1/2, and 1 cup.

Liquid measuring cups are used to measure the volume of a liquid ingredient such as water, milk, whipping cream, or oil. Liquid measuring cups most times come with a pour spout and cup, fluid ounces, milliliter, pint, quart, gallon, liter measurements on the side of the cups. (See next page)

Dry Measurements conversions:

Imperial (U.S.)	Metric (UK)
1 ounce	28 grams
2 ounces	55 grams
3 ounces	85 grams
4 ounces	115 grams
8 ounces	225 grams
16 ounces	455 grams

DRY MEASUREMENTS

1 Cup = 16 Tablespoons
1 pound dry = 16 ounces

LIQUID CONVERSIONS

SMALL VOLUME (LIQUID) :

TABLESPOONS / CUPS / FLUID OUNCES

1 Tablespoon = 3 teaspoons = 1/2 fluid ounce
2 Tablespoons = 1/8 cup = 1 fluid ounce
4 Tablespoons = 1/4 cup = 2 fluid ounces
5 Tablespoons + 1 teaspoon = 1/3 cup
16 Tablespoons = 1 cup = 8 fluid ounces

LARGE VOLUME (LIQUID) :

CUPS / FLUID OUNCES / PINTS / QUARTS / GALLONS

1 cup = 8 fluid ounces = 1/2 pint
2 cups = 16 fluid ounces = 1 pint =1/2 quart
3 cups = 24 fluid ounces = 1 1/2 pints
4 cups = 32 fluid ounces = 2 pints =1 quart
8 cups = 64 fluid ounces = 2 quarts =1/2 gallon
16 cups = 128 fluid ounces = 4 quarts =1 gallon

IMPERIAL (U.S.) / METRIC (UK) / (AU)

1/4 tsp. = 1 ml. = 1 ml.
1/2 tsp. = 2 ml. = 2 ml.
1 tsp. = 5 ml. = 5 ml.
1 Tbsp. = 15 ml. = 20 ml.
1/4 cup = 50 ml. = 50 ml.
1/3 cup = 75 ml. = 75 ml.
1/2 cup = 125 ml. = 125 ml.
2/3 cup = 150 ml. = 150 ml.
3/4 cup = 175 ml. = 175 ml.
1 cup = 250 ml. = 250 ml.
1 pint = 500 ml. = 625 ml.
1 quart = 1 liter = 1 liter

Measurement may differ at different regions of the world.

For example; In Australia(AU), 1 pint = 20 fl. oz. or 2-1/2 cups

TEMPERATURE CONVERSIONS

Fahrenheit (°F)	Celsius (°C)	Description	Gas Mark
32°	0°	-	
212°	100°	-	
250°	120°	-	1/2
275°	140°	Cool	1
300°	150°	-	2
325°	160°	Very Moderate	3
350°	180°	Moderate	4
375°	190°	-	5
400°	200°	Moderately Hot	6
425°	220°	Hot	7
450°	230°	-	8
475°	240°	Very Hot	9
500°	260°		

QUICK COOKING REFERENCE

Low Heat
\>225°F to 249°F
(107°C to 120°C)

Boiling, Simmering and Poaching. Also used for holding items warm.

Oils Smoke Points:
Unrefined Canola Oil
Unrefined Flaxseed Oil

Medium / Low Heat
250°F to 324°F
(121°C to 161°C)

Slower cooking line leaner meats, stew, stocks and reductions

Oils Smoke Points:
Unrefined Corn Oil
Unrefined Flaxseed Oil

Medium Heat
325°F to 374°F
(162°C to 189°C)

Simmer or reduction, Cook food all the way through

Oils Smoke Points:
Hemp Seed Oil
Extra Virgin Olive Oil
Butter

Medium/High Heat
375°F to 449°F
(190°C to 231°C)

Pan Frying, Searing

Oils Smoke Points:
Macadamia Nut Oil
Refined Canola Oil

High Heat
450°F to 650°F
(232°C to 343°C)

Saute, Grilling, Pan Roasting

Oils Smoke Points:
Refined Peanut Oil
Refined Sunflower Oil

NOTES PAGE

NOTES PAGE

INDEX

INDEX

A
APPETIZERS 13
APPETIZERS, SALAD
Arugula Salad 17
Dill Chicken Salad with Pomegranate Vinaigrette 16
Herb Salad 15
Roasted beets salad with macadamia vinaigrette 15

APPETIZERS - SNACKS 24
Roasted mini sweet peppers 28
Sautéed Medjool Dates with Sea Salt 26
Spiced Marcona 24

APPETIZERS - SOUP 18
Butternut Squash 21
Mussel Soup 22
Roasted Butternut Squash Soup 20
Strawberry Gazpacho 18

B
Bacon, Capers, Braised Green Flat bread 46
Basmati Rice 53
Bechamel sauce 77
Braised Lamb with Israeli Couscous 54
Braised Green 46
Brine Recipe 76
Broth 23
Butternut Squash 21

C
Candied Pecans 77

Caramelized onions 77
Chocolate Mousse 70

Conversions Liquids 83
Conversions Temperature 84

Creme Brulee Chocolate Mousse 70
Creme Fraiche 77
Crispy Skin Salmon with Roasted Asparagus Salad 62
Croutons 37

D
Danish Butter Cookie 69
DESSERTS 65
DESSERTS- SWEETS 66
Passion Fruit Soufflé with Pear Passion Sauce 66
Cardamom Ice Cream with Danish Butter Cookie 68
Creme Brulee 70
Mojito Sorbet 71

G
Garlic Broccoli and Brussels Sprouts 36
Gazpacho 19

I
Israeli Couscous 55

M
Macadamia Nut Vinaigrette 15
MAIN DISHES 49
MAIN DISHES - MEATS AND POULTRY 50
Braised Lamb with Israeli Couscous 54
Passion Glazed Pork Belly with Potato Gnocchi 50

Tandoori Chicken with Basmati Rice 52

MAIN DISHES - SEAFOOD 60
Crispy Skin Salmon with Roasted Asparagus Salad 62

Pan-Seared Trout with Horseradish Risotto 60

MAIN DISHES - VEGETARIAN 56
Open-Faced Tomato Pea Pesto Sandwich 58
Stuffed Mushroom Eggplant Caps 56

Mojito Sorbet 71
Mussel Soup 22

O
Open-Faced Tomato Pea Pesto Sandwich 58

P
Passion Fruit Soufflé with Pear Passion Sauce 66
Passion Glazed Pork Belly with Potato Gnocchi 50
Potato Gnocchi 78
Pear Passion Sauce 67
Pickled Red Onions 78
Pomegranate Vinaigrette 17
Potato Gnocchi 78
Prosciutto, Figs, and capers 32

R
REFRESHER 71
Mojito Sorbet 71

Roasted Beets Salad with Macadamia Nut Vinaigrette 14
Roasted mini sweet peppers 28

Q
Quick cooking Reference 85

S
Sautéed Medjool Dates with Sea Salt 26
Spiced Marcona 24
Seafood Paella 42
Seared Ahi Tuna with Passion Vinaigrette 40

SMALL PLATES 31
SMALL PLATES - MEATS 44
Bacon, Capers, Braised Green Flat bread 46
Pan-Seared Sliced Beef with Green Peas 44

SMALL PLATES - SEAFOOD 40
Seared Ahi Tuna with Passion Vinaigrette 40

SMALL PLATES -VEGETARIAN 36
Garlic Broccoli and Brussels Sprouts 36
Tomato Avocado Salad 38
Stuffed Mushroom Eggplant Caps 56

SUB RECIPES 73
Brine Recipe 76
Candied Pecans 77
Caramelized onions 77
Creme Fraiche 77
Pickled Red Onions 78
Potato Gnocchi 78

T
Tandoori Chicken with Basmati Rice 52
Tomato Avocado Salad 38
Tomato Bruschetta 34

W
White Chicken Stock 74
White Vegetable Stock 75

"Where It all began"

A hidden Gem in the Pacific NW

Trip to the Markets in France - lots of offal

Venice Italy - Risotto with black squid ink very popular.

Izmir, Turkey - Kebaps are a must try

On the hills above Bacharach in Germany

SPECIAL THANKS

Special thanks to my parents, siblings, and the entire Green family - coach "are you done yet."

All other photos contained in this book are from my own private collection and archives.

Deserving a heartfelt thank you are my Professional Mentors, Chefs and Military Service members & Veterans. All of whom took their time to teach others, follow their passion, and mentor always.